HOW TO HAVE A THREESOME

(OR IF YOU'RE A LOSER, HOW TO GET JUST ONE)

MICHAEL SCOTT GRANT

CONTENTS

I wrote this therapeutic resource originally in 2007, and I want to recognize that certain elements may not be as palpable in today's Me Too era. Mutual respect is and always has been the cornerstone of the activities described in this guide, and none of those activities would have resulted in the absence of it.

Additionally, I'm cognizant that, from today's perspective, some of the humor seem so stale that a necrophiliac tried to hump them. However, I left it unfiltered because it's truthful, something missing lately. If there's one thing we've learned about the past these last four years, it's that some people deserve to be left in it. Surround yourself with successful, optimistic people who are smarter than you are, and listen to them for once. No self-improvement = no sex improvement.

So happy hunting, boys and girls. Many safe opportunities await you after it's safe to rip that mask off and kiss a total stranger.

Now that most of us are showing only 25% of our faces, you really need to connect on an emotional level, more so than was true in 2007. It's okay that you're on your own path. And post-COVID, we're all gonna have a lot of sex together, and these are the blueprints. You know, why risk it on just one spreader? Remember, when she wants you to, talk dirty to her, and somewhere an angel loses their wings.

INTRODUCTION

Merriam-Webster's dictionary doesn't have a definition for "threesome," but if it did, it would go something like this: "woo woo woo, ruff ruff ruff, nyah nyah nyah, ahhooooogah."

I'm out looking for some nick nack paddy whack in suburban Detroit. She's wearing a corset-type top, and her clevelands are jacked up just under her chin. It's dark, but I think I saw the tops of her stockings. Even her shoes mean business, with one dangling on her toe, bouncing until it falls away. While sliding it back on, her knees pop open enough to reveal a Brazilian peeking out. She catches me looking, and I nervously wink (while my cock struggles to get out of its cage in my pants). She sorta smiles at me, then accosts me. "Listen, my husband said if you don't stop staring at my vagina, he's gonna do some de-constructive surgery on your face."

I swallow as she turns and walks away. He's across the bar, football big and staring at me. A moment later, he's in my mix. "Hey, dude," he says to me, paralyzing me in my spot. He has this look in his eyes, but he vanishes into the bathroom, passing me by.

No sooner does she pop back up out of nowhere than she whispers in my ear, "If you want to fuck that pussy you just saw, my husband said come over in twenty minutes." She adds, "Do you remember where we live?"

I nod yes as she takes my hand and makes me feel her wetness from the inside of her skirt. She's soaking. She's such a whore. That's why her husband and I treat her like a queen. If she was a bitchy queen, then you'd treat her like a whore. But a queen would never have a threesome anyway. They like their control and attention undivided.

So I go to their mansion for the second time, unable to resist her beauty and allure. Now inside, I find myself in their halfway, looking at pictures of the three children whose mother I'm about to defile in front of their father. Welcome to the world of the ménage à trois. In other words, **_if it starts to get weird ... you're there_**.

The three most frequent questions I get are:

1. Where do you go to meet them?
2. What do you say to convince them?
3. What kind of "stuff" did they do?

The answer to all of these questions is yes ... yes, the answers are in this book.

When it comes to dating hot guys, women spend a lot of time in their closets, figuring out what they won't be wearing at the end of the night. The funny thing is that most "hot guys" go home alone because they can't communicate, so losers like me get the women. Because threesomes happen to normal guys. If you can't get one on your own, I'll improve your odds. If you're more advanced, I'll have you advancing even more.

Remember, you aren't just sleeping with her. You're sleeping with everyone she has ever slept with. So **_good news_**, losers, your numbers just went way up because we're gonna meet some sluts.

So who's a loser? Everyone. No soul has escaped scrutiny, ridicule, criticism, rejection, harassment, avoidance, isolation, or confrontation. My last girlfriend called me a loser (after being in love for a whole year). My high school crush called me a reject. My buddies all call me a dork and a fag. Whatever. I never let it get me down, even though I know it's true (except the fag part—I'm straight and always have been). I have above-average looks, but I think I'm just average, and that makes me approachable.

I know I'm not a loser, any more than you think you are or any woman out there thinks she is. A loser is someone who doesn't try anymore. Reading this is a sign that you're willing to participate in the story of your life, which I wouldn't want to read ... so far. But that can be changed.

You know if you're out in a blizzard on a Wednesday night in your small backwards-ass town, it can only be for a few reasons: to get **drunk** and/or **laid**. So the rest of you families, get out of our way. We're **horny**!

Going out to get women is a numbers game. Having a threesome is a lottery win. You can't change luck. It's tied to fate. But you can improve your chances with the implementation of the strategies and techniques I outline for you so you can gain an advantage.

To help you, I broke this book down into the easiest format known to man: who, what, where, when, how, and during. There's no why because if you have to ask why, then **goodbye**. But, actually, there is a section about the whycology of group sex.

So why me? I'm qualified. I'm an aficionado—I think. I've been in a dozen or so threesomes, seduced more than 200 women, had nine best girlfriends, written three screenplays, penned two sitcoms, authored several treatments on spec, and earned a degree in film marketing with a minor in psychology and advertising. Oh yeah, and I'm an executive producer at an adult video production company. I'm a ***very***, ***very***, ***very***, ***very***, ***lucky*** man.

I shoot audition screen tests. Conservative friends and associates are critical of that enterprise, so I tell 'em, "Look, if you don't like porn, you just have a stick up your ass, which, by the way, *is porn!*"

Modeling has changed. Pornography isn't stigmatized like it was in previous generations. Now it's funny and educational. So whether I'm advocating for a nineteen-year-old actress to try the anal scene or talking a husband into letting me share his wife, it's all about respect for the woman. If a woman feels secure, adored, loved, and safe, then she'll do anything (SOURCE: Every woman in the world).

Because I'm a man, I hate reading, so I wrote this as short as possible. I also insisted that it be cheap enough to throw out the window should your significant other catch you reading it. So if you're ready to roll, here's rule #1: There are no rules. So how can you lose?

Let's get it done! Done like an only son!

1

HOW: SO YOU WANT A LITTLE "NICK NACK PADDY WHACK"?

Step 1 – Meet new woman.
Step 2 – Add up measurements. If greater
than 100, repeat Step 1.

WHEN YOU WALK in the door, do you own it? Or do you avoid attention and try to blend in? Does everyone checking you out see fear or confidence in your eyes? What do you focus on when entering a new place? Do you go right to the bar?

Your entrance will make/break your chances of a successful evening at that venue, and your opening lines and successive banter will contribute to the longevity of each new relationship you form through flirting. Instead of using a cheesy line like, "Is there a map to your head? 'Cause I'm lost in your eyes," try a charming line like, "When you smile, your whole face smiles."

If she shoots you down, don't worry. You'll never again see about 98% of the people you meet in your life, so treat it like practice. Technically, nobody ever really rejects you. They're all merely practice for the real thing, which will happen when you finally stop looking for it, ironically.

Although your approach begins long before your entrance (namely, during prep work), now is the time to circle the wagons or "perimeter-ize"—positioning yourself on the outer fringe without acknowledging you're there. Quickly scan for the most approachable, average women, preferably without guys (competition) around them, and insert your ass into their group space. Ignore them initially by keeping turned away, and have a grand conversation with your wingman, who keeps you laughing and smiling so that if one of them scans you, it's while you're looking good and having fun. Be coy about eye contact. If there's lots of chemistry, there will be a lot of eye contact between you two later.

When your wingman signals that you have a qualified group, tum and deliver an opening pick-up line like one of the following (ultimately, though, your ice breaker should be tailored to that individual, at that moment in time, and unique to that microcosm):

- "Hello, ladies. No mullet, no lazy eye, no cold sores…. How am I doin' so far?"
- "Hi, ladies. Wow, you all look so hot tonight. As a designer, I hate that! I have nothing to criticize."
- "Let's do shots. It's my birthday … later this year."

Seems easy, right? Well you only have two minutes to get in, charm 'em, and get out The more you wait, the more you masturbate. This technique is called the "Hit & Run."

Women don't like *Star Trek*, so don't be a Cling-On. Offer something unique while testing your compatibility with the alpha female (usually the tallest and prettiest in the group), but don't neglect the betas guarding her. Adjust if necessary, and switch your attention to a beta, then get the hell out of there.

I like to leave on a funny, high note. I might say, "Watch my drink. I don't want the busboy to take it away. I already put the roofies in it. … Hey, it's a long, boring drive home, and I don't like remembering it."

If you were charming, sincere, and unique, they will want to talk to you more. But you want to create the perception that you're busy, popular, and in demand—hard to get, like women used to be. Because women are used to getting what they want, when you deny them, they feel challenged and will chase down that opportunity.

And what do I mean by "unique"?

- You just saved someone's life recently.
- You're an artist.
- You dated a celebrity.
- You have a new scar and a story.
- You just had a threesome last month.

You don't have to meet everyone in the venue and look desperate (when it comes to flirting, that's like having the plague), but try to smile at everyone, even if they don't reciprocate.

Nobody is out of your league, so hit on a full array of women, not just your "type." But let the miserable ones be. They'll wind up sitting on a sex toy by themselves tonight anyway. Resist the urge to lash out at her if she shuts you down during your opener or disses you in front of her friends. No, feel pity for her. She's angry and missing something if she has to get off on making fun of your unpretentious ass. But if you can't, then make sure the whole bar hears you when you reply, "Yeah, I'll call you ... call you a whore to all our friends."

Now on to the plan-B women. Find another area away from the "A" women and re-cultivate. Initiate with new eye candy and approach within one to four minutes of that flush of serotonin. If not, you blew it. Women don't like being undressed with your eyes, which is slang for over-staring. They believe you're only interested in their chests if you don't follow up with conversation. So don't be a mannequin, never blinking and freaking her out and such.

Flirting is simply listening and having something to say back to the stranger you want to fuck the hell out of. Flattery is so obvious, so use charm instead.

"Red is your color. You're *schmoking* in that dress."

While she responds to a compliment, look her in the eyes and avoid scanning the room. Make her feel like she's the only one in there with you. Tilt your head ever so slightly to the side while perceptibly nodding and—this is important—shut up. If she doesn't respond, try something that will get her attention.

Women desire adoration, especially when they're in the middle of an estrogenic competition. If you scan the room when you're talking to a beta, you're implying that you're bored. It also signals that you're looking for something better. It's anti-foundation laying. Don't do it. Generally, I avoid touching women first as well. Express yourself through eye contact, tone, hand gestures, and body language, which includes your smile. Let her break the personal space barrier by leaning in to repeat something she said in your ear after you repeatedly—and intentionally—asked, "What?"

If you must make boob jokes, make them about anybody in the bar but the woman you're speaking with. You might say something like, "Look at that outfit. She doesn't know a thing about advertising." She'll feel neglected, causing her to over-compensate to your benefit. Once she's there, go further and see if you can get a finger in her mouth. If she sucks it, you're doing well. If she bites it off, leaving a bloodied metacarpal, repeat.

Step 1 – Find a woman. Add up her measurements ...

Being silly in the context of obscurity can be confusing to women, who are born categorizers. Always leave her guessing about what you're going to say next. When you say a word with "L" in it, roll your tongue over your lips in circles while making the "lllll" sound. "LLLLLook out llllladies. It's LLLLLori LLLLLoughllllin." Then make a fist, extend your index finger, and bend it into a "C," then hook it into your mouth like a largemouth bass, and suck in air (like you're in the dentist's chair), implying that she makes you drool. You can also make the subject one of the women you just met to imply your attraction to her effectively but without much subtlety or pressure. It's called a sight gag in comedy, and it rarely fails to elicit laughter, to captivate attention in a hostile crowd (they all feel hostile when you get back into the dating scene), and to grant you extra real estate for continued flirting.

The irony is that no matter how much you make her laugh, you must balance that with being a jerk. Women get hit on all day by losers who tell them, "You're so pretty." They want someone different to challenge them. They respond to what I coined the "Cloak & Dagger Compliment" (see "Techniques"), which is designed to work in conjunction with "The Chase." It should leave them wondering whether you just paid them a compliment or an insult (it was both). Did they just get played?

Keep 'em laughing instead. I used to write one-liners and fire them off in rapid succession so they could barely catch their breath from laughing.

- "I'm in a sex addicts class. ... I'm trying to learn how to become one."
- "I invented the Pez dispenser for adults. It comes in three flavors: Prozac, Viagra, and Tums."

I've been a comedian in Hollywood for years, and I've had jokes on the late-night talk shows. Then I became a porn producer. No matter my profession, it has always been about being funny. But nothing is as important as being respectful. When it comes to threesomes, that's especially true. Well, not after. It's about being glad you all drove separate cars sometimes. Sometimes it's about being glad.

Overview of Strategies

1. Hit & Run
2. Faux Set-Up
3. Lacking Experience
4. Wingman/Wingbirds
5. Position of Authority
6. Treat Her Like Shit
7. Gay or Not?
8. Jealousy
9. I'm Waiting for the Right Two

Overview of Techniques

a. The Chase
b. Cloak & Dagger Compliment
c. Alcohol & Drugs
d. Drop Bomb / Change Subject
e. Fear of Missing Out on Orgies (FOMOO)
f. I Can't Choose
g. Titillation Talk
h. Fear of Something

Hit & Run

Hit & Run is the best, most proven strategy for breeding familiarity in groups of unestablished strangers (SOURCE:

Men). The key is to make a great but quick first impression, one that always leaves them wanting more. Two minutes in and out on the first "hit," five minutes on the second hit, and on the third, you can move into their SUV. Or at the very least, you can get more time to apply the strategies and techniques that improve your odds of achieving the #1 male fantasy of all time:

> To catch a game-winning Super Bowl touchdown pass while simultaneously banging two cheerleaders—a busty Asian dressed like Wonder Woman and a USC co-ed in a Princess Leia outfit, chain collar included.

It works for those of you who fear rejection more than usual because it forces you out of there before you get too nervous and say something stupid like, "Are those real?" Instead, you build a resistance that's easy to digest in small bites until there's an appetite for more. With each successful visit, you build confidence for the next encounter. If you "return a victor," say, with shots for everyone or VIP passes or something **unique**, you've ensured a soft landing for the third hit, as long as you don't overstay your welcome during the second hit. Move on. And don't plant your seeds all in one hole. Spread them out so the garden is lush and bushy (NOTE: If you get flat out turned down, **do not re-hit**. She weeded herself out for you, thereby preventing you from wasting your time weeding her out. We want to be eating it out, not weeding it out, right?)

The group you perimeter-ize yourself on will be watching to see who you like most. Half the fun is not letting them know which one until later. They all think they have a chance with me. That way I likely won't get blockage for my cockage from any of them later, when I'm finally choosing one (or two). Each woman deserves the schmooze (that's not slang for semen. It means to kiss butt without being transparent, for those of you in the South).

On your second run, have your wingman remove you, this time by whispering something in your ear. It looks official. It creates curiosity and still leaves them wanting more. Like Kim Kardashian and anything edible.

On the third hit, **you** are that funny or cute guy who keeps leaving, but finally you can realize the real estate you have developed and pick and choose combinations of strategies, lines, and techniques to get some after-hours lovin'. Use too many at once, and you'll appear desperate, hungry, and creepy, but mostly just pathetic. Like Kim Kardashian and anything edible.

During this stage, I'd employ either a surprise hit or drop the bomb and change the subject. You should kiss her within one to two hours of this approach. It takes the pressure off the goodnight kiss later because the first kiss is already out of the way, leading to a make-out session in lieu of a peck on the cheek. The timing is best when you share a moment, when she gives you "the look," or when she says something that you both believe in passionately. "Oh my God. I hate Kim Kardashian too!"

MWAH. On the lips, no tongue, two seconds maximum, when she's not expecting it. And wink afterward. I admit that I'm fast. I mean, I won't even take a woman out to dinner unless she's let me visit Bra-land. Why waste money? Dating is different from having a girlfriend. Now if someone asks me out and they pay, I'll probably fuck her. Yep. I'll fuck her for a Happy Meal.

Or you can drop the bomb if things aren't touchy-feely yet. "If I died tomorrow, I'd still be happy with my short life ... I just had my first threesome last week with women I met here." Then don't bring it up again for hours, even if she lobs many questions at you.

"Wing-birds" are wingmen who have boobies. Having a wing-bird will get you laid three times more often than hunting with another single guy and ten times more often than hunting by yourself. Put up with what it takes to be friends with hot women: drama, insecurities, selfishness, entitlement, and spacey-ness because hot women, like Monte Carlo slots, pay off. How so?

- A hot woman can make other betas around her do nearly anything.
- She can play the phony jealousy card when you flirt.
- She can divert unwelcome male competition from you and the woman you've set your sights on.
- She provides an energy people want to be around, putting you in contact with other alphas you might never have thought you could get.
- You can score points off her. "No, she's just my friend. So pretty, but no self-esteem. What a shame, huh?"
- A hot woman will be invited to continue partying elsewhere. Everywhere elsewhere.
- She can feed the woman you want a wheelbarrow-full of disinformation, propaganda, etc. "We had a threesome last year. I think he could have even handled one more." Or less salacious, "He broke up with me," leaving her to wonder.

The perception is that you're safe and stable and that you hang around babes all the time. But if she's on the market too, don't mess up your wing-bird's game with possessiveness, lingering, jealousy, or machismo. The best birds already have a man, so there's no confusion about your "working relation-ship" with her. Plus, she will concentrate on helping you close the deal. But the hotter the woman, the higher the drama. I'm not saying my ex-girlfriend was a drama queen, but they did offer her a role on *Housewives of Detroit*. ... All of them. ... All at once.

Faux Set-Up

"Faux Set-Up" is a great strategy to use on a beta. In your second or third hit, ask her who she likes in the bar or on the beach or wherever you are. Now here's the trick: teach her Hit & Run as I taught you. It will fail by design. Because it's designed for men, not women. Women are nesters, which means they let shit come to them. Men are hunters—we go to the shit. Once she's briefed, send her off to go flirt with guys you know will turn her down. After striking out over and over, you become her soft landing, all sympathetic and ready to give her a consoling hug. Then a drink. Then a compliment to boost her ego. Then a surprise kiss after you both joke that he's gay. Tell her, "Aw, that's okay. There's a number you can call for that ... mine." (TIP: Find out if her faux target is interested in her or not [in the men's room]. You can only sabotage what you know about [SOURCE: All married couples].)

Lacking Experience

"Lacking Experience" is a niche strategy that only works in certain situations. It's geared toward a long-term outcome. A bad boy is more apt to pull this off than a loser. It's commonly used on younger women who are stingy about putting out or who are sexually repressed. After sex or heavy foreplay, you can tell her something like this: "I like you and all, but I just don't think you're experienced enough for me." You can deviously add, "It's okay. That's just how you are. There's nothing wrong with that. Everyone moves at their own pace. I just want someone more secure with her body." It can be devastating to a woman to hear that, and she will be back one day to prove you wrong. It could be months or even years until you see her again, but if she lets you nail her, savor the slutiness as she proves you wrong over and over and over.

It can also be used to encourage a re-match (an extension of a one-night stand). Women like a challenge and an opportunity to validate themselves. For example, you might say something like, "That was amazing. No debating that. But it felt like you were holding back, like your body was all tense. But you were probably just nervous. I'm sure you don't always suck in bed."

Position of Authority

"Position of Authority" (POA) is meant for established couples, alpha-beta power ladders, and "Beauty and the Geek" relationships. One of the people in the relationship says, "Honey, we're having a threesome," and the other complies. If the POA is negatively driven by fear, intimidation, coercion, shame, guilt, or violence, then it won't be conducive to a fulfilling encounter. On the other hand, if the

POA is the wife, then what other tools besides fear, intimidation, coercion, shame, and guilt does she have? Uh oh. I'm gonna get in trouble for that one.

Whether it's the man or the woman, the POA should be used in a loving way. Many of the above diversions are anti-intimacy, which leads us to the strategy that has been around longer than any other strategy known to man—cave or modern.

Treat Her Like Shit

"Treat Her Like Shit" only works half the time. The other half of the time, it doesn't work. Know why? You can only treat a queen like shit. She's used to *everyone* kissing her tight little ass. Treat her like garbage and she'll magically respond. Screwed up, huh? Yep. This is going to be foreign to some of you momma's boys, but the song is true: you have to be cruel to be kind. If you fall in love and say it first too fast, you'll get fired. If Frosty the Snow Bitch senses sensitivity in you, she'll find someone else to play with. Bad boys understand this seemingly illogical juxtaposition and, thus, get laid more than you do. Trust me. Get used to getting slapped in the face. It means you're pushing the buttons necessary to evoke the passion and emotion in women that returns results.

Even strong, independent, and beautiful women ask me, "What's with all this respect crap you write about? Can't it just be degrading, dirty sex?" The answer is that it can be, you bag of trash, as long as it's mutual.

Is He Gay?

"Is He Gay?" is what metrosexuals hear a lot in the field form women they're working. I use it to my advantage because women love non-threatening homosexuals. A lover once said to me, "I thought you were gay until you had me against the wall, toes pointing north and south."

You can just dabble a little by saying "honey" before you begin a criticism of her. Throw in some comments about their shoes, and she'll love you and be confused. It's also effective for disarming other guys in the crowd. They will misinterpret you as harmless as you woo away their bored babes. Use conversation-ending words like, "Super!" Tell people you're straight if they ask. If you're not straight, then go with bi. If you're not bi, then you may be confused about this book.

Jealousy as a Motivator

"Jealousy as a Motivator" is for the more experienced players. It involves juggling a few women at a time, and perhaps you even have a choice between several on occasion. The simplest way to use what salespeople call the "standing room only" theory is to be looking at your top choice while a plan-B or even C woman is draped all over you. It's your way of telling her, *If I'm not fucking you in thirty minutes, I'm fucking her.* It's the old "shit or get off the fence" mixed metaphor.

I'm Waiting for the Right Two

"I'm Waiting for the Right Two"—does this bullshit line even need explaining?

Techniques

The Chase

The Chase is the basis of attraction. It's something women in previous decades preferred before the revolution of sexuality that ensued after Roe v. Wade and, more recently, a sitcom called *Sex and the...* something, I forget. Thanks to the equality movement, women have an appreciable amount of power on top the power of the pussy. They want to stalk prey and get a taste of our male killer instincts for their own satisfaction. You can turn the tables on the sexual roles.

Because of your uniqueness, because you can dish it out and take it, or maybe because you have money, you're hard to get. Not impossible though. You have to let her know that you're just for fun and kind of hard to handle. You propose that she's better off with some pin-dick accountant she can manipulate.

You be bad. Say something like, "Yo, I don't wanna fuck down with you, but we can just kick it."

Well, well, well. No female is about to listen to someone saying he doesn't want to fuck down with her. If you're still hanging out with her in two weeks, she should be intravenously attached to your Woodrow Wilson.

Cloak & Dagger Compliment

The Cloak & Dagger Compliment is a complement to The Chase. Notice the disparate use of spellings to convey the distinct separation between that which is flattering in the former and that which accompanies something else nicely in the latter.

What did you notice about that last sentence? It's time to start using the brain and all those big words stored up there. Without sounding like a pompous ass, you should try to arrange your words so they showcase your intelligence, not your emotions. You have to have the right kind of attitude to smack down a Cloak & Dagger on a pretty woman. It's not for the squeamish. But gauge her response, and you'll learn a lot about her. Here are some examples:

Cool

"Women all look the same lately in the club, with their trendy makeup, bookworm glasses, and matching Louis Vuitton purses. So why wouldn't I pick the one in ten who isn't a bitch? Like you."

Cold

"That dress is good for you. It hides your fat ass."

Frozed Out

"Hey, you can't blame a guy for trying for a 9. I mean a Michigan 9, which is like a New York 3 or an LA 4. ... But, hey, we aren't in LA."

Alcohol and Drugs

Alcohol and drugs are two reasons that men and women get together, even though they're diametrically opposed beings wired completely differently and totally bent on sabotage and misery.

Spirits—readily available, easily persuasiveable, made to your specifications. You get the picture (I'm making up words). Yeah, booze is fun. And it sure helps tum off those busy brains that plague women. But remember this: underage girls who drink in the bar are the bar's problem. But if you supply them, it's your problem. That's illegal in most states.

And remember this too:

Too much alcohol for you = Sleep
Too much alcohol for her = Rape

Some community professionals might frown on the use of substances to catalyze an orgy, but they're just jealous because they were too ugly to be invited to one in the '40s, when they grew up. The sobering news is that alcohol was responsible for 75% of my threesomes. That's also the good news. God bless the bottle. It was responsible for my threesomes!

Drop the Bomb / Change the Subject

"Drop the Bomb / Change the Subject," as mentioned earlier, is a sure-fire technique to arouse mild suspicion, curiosity, and mystique in a liberal audience. Saying something like this should do the trick: "Two weeks ago, I had a threesome with women I met in this very bar. Why do you think I came back, for that white corned beef sandwich they serve here?"

Later on, you can stoke their curiosity by describing it in plush, sordid detail. But avoid the subject at first, like you never even brought it up. Suspense, like their buzz, will be heightened in another sixty minutes.

Fear of Missing Out on Orgies (FOMOO)

"Fear of Missing Out on Orgies (FOMOO)" is starting to get whiny and needy, but it creates cognitive dissonance in an active mind that's always wondering if it's missing out on something. "You've got to just try it once. I mean, why not? I could understand if you were some guy who couldn't get any, but you're a beautiful woman. Even if you don't do it with me, you owe yourself the pleasure of doubling your pleasure." You can also add on something like, "Just because you do it once doesn't mean you have to do it again. You're not obligated to run for 'Swing Queen.'"

I Can't Choose

"I Can't Choose" is what you say if you've netted two interested, qualified women and both seem like they might both go home and share ya. Try something like the following line, delivered with just the right amount of sarcasm: "I can't choose between you because you're both such good kissers and beautiful, smart ladies. ... The only solution is for me to sacrifice myself to each of you sexually ... simultaneously ... which I'll do, this one time only ... for free."

Titillation Talk

"Titillation Talk" is dirty conversation you have with the woman you've set your sights on. It's a turn-on that leads to romance. Sometimes I'll try to guess what color her nipples are—brown or pink, depending on whether she's a brunette or a blonde. She'll usually tease you and tell you or maybe even show you one to prove that you're right or (her preference) that you're wrong.

Recently I was talking in the club with my friend Jerry and two older women. One said she was wearing a minimizer bra because her tits were so heavy. Her girlfriend agreed, squeezing them like the oil companies squeeze us, only harder. Then she invited us guys to cop a feel, saying, "See?" I wasted no time, grabbing a handful and bouncing that sweater meat up and down like a juggler.

The moral is this: get what you can. Despite their official position, women love sex, foreplay, and being sexually exhilarated by interesting men. Nightclubs are dark so they can be naughty without the illumination of judgement on them.

Afraid of Something

"Afraid of Something" is the hard-sell technique. Fear of the unknown can be crippling. It can also be enlightening and empowering once you master it. Surmise which of these types of fear she harbors, then alleviate it by overcoming objections.

- Fear of what people might say about you when they find out that you're what, a slut?

  Big deal. Sluts get what they want.

- Fear of being hurt, being used.

  Uh, you mean like everyone is?

- Fear of regretting your impulsiveness or being ashamed of it

  *Not if you pick the right kind of people (i.e., **no** "glossies").*

- Fear that you might have a heart attack.

  Me too. I should be dead seven times over by now.

- Fear you might like it too much.

  Probably, but you'll never know until you try it.

- Fear you'll go "lez."

I didn't.

- Fear Jesus won't have you in heaven with God.

So what. You know how those single-parent families are anyway.

The best way to avoid the games that come with interpersonal relationships is to do the prep work beforehand so your mind is sharp and your physique is toned.

Prep

Let's talk about prep, baby. Let's talk about therapy. Let's talk about all the good things and the bad things like acne. Let's talk about prep.

Women have their own money these days, so that's not the only motivator for going out to meet guys. They want hot, toe-curling young studs. Having a threesome is like an haute couture (high fashion) photo shoot. Nobody recalls all the prep work that went into it. They just remember the final shot ... on her face.

Speaking of gushy orgasms and high fashion, now is a good time to begin reading up on your adversaries. Magazines like *Vogue*, *Cosmopolitan*, *Mademoiselle*, and *Elle* (French for "she") will give you insights into the female psyche, will help you determine their motivations, and will equip you with the ability to deconstruct their strategies. Women read our magazines so they know what we're up to (*Playboy* has a 50% female readership), so why shouldn't you do the same?

Men don't need to "glam up" like women do, but you should have a skin, teeth, and hair regime every day. Skin likes routine, so follow a plan the same time every day using the appropriately recommended products in the right combination. MAC cosmetics has a great line for men. They're expensive but impressive. When a woman gets in the shower with you afterward and sees MAC, she knows she can wash **everything** off her face with that brand.

Hair, conversely, likes it switched up. Follicles need to be stimulated, so change product constantly. Pert one day, Paul Mitchell the next, a conditioner on the third day, especially if you swim. What I'm saying is that you shouldn't just be yourself! Be someone better.

Here's what it costs to prep for a threesome:

$25 - Teeth whitening (Crest strips, 7-day premium)

$20 - Facial cleanser (MAC counter at Macy's)

$40 - Rogaine (pharmacy, no prescription)

$20 - Paul Mitchell (salons or department store)

$1 - Dental floss (grocery store)

Total $106

Tell me if that hundred bucks didn't make a difference in your appearance over thirty days.

Don't go shopping for clothes by yourself unless you really have your own style. How would *you* know that your ass looks good in certain jeans or that your package looks very "grabbable" in a pair of dress pants? The best time to shop is when you have a girlfriend. Let her pick out your clothes because she's the one that has to sleep with you. Wear whatever she says, especially if you hate it. The older you get, the more you'll appreciate this. If I know women, that shirt you hate in the store will become your "lucky" outfit when you both are broken up down the road.

Wherever you're getting your hair cut, ***stop*** going there. I know you like that little cosmetologist who cuts your hair while sticking her big knockers in your face in the salon in the mall, but if she's giving you a bad cut, what exactly are you paying her for? A great stylist cuts every piece of hair, and it could take a full hour if done correctly. Find a gay hairstylist or get referrals for upscale salons so your hair is done right. Unless you have the low-class gangster buzzcut like all the felons in prison. Then you can just use a Flowbee, killer.

The more you shit, the lighter you get—that's the mantra for losing weight. Most of us need to drop 5% to 20% of our bodyweight. A painless way to do so is with the new fiber products you put into your sports drink, your yogurt, or your orange juice. You'll crap cables, I swear. The fiber is tasteless, odorless, and not gritty. You'll wish you could say the same about threesomes.

Ever get a facial? No, not a money shot into her eyes and hair like the pornos. I'm talking about a spa facial. Pore cleansing, exfoliation, and moisturization lead to clean skin. Face it, no one wants you going down on them with a pimply face. Same with your nails. You don't get fingered as a guy, so you don't notice fingers. But women do. Dirty fingernails = yeast infection. Oily, black hands = yeast infection. I'm told they're no fun. So get the freakin' manicure.

Glasses are an overlooked accessory for men. I own a pair of Gucci glasses that have no prescription lenses in them (I have better than 20/20 vision). Vain, you say? Yeah, sure. But I purchased them because I thought they made the bump in my nose less apparent and gave me an air of sophistication. I look almost doctorly, which increases my credibility. It took a year to find just the right pair. I also have colored contact lenses that are mainly for fun. Every little bit helps when trying to keep up with the competition.

Jewelry is an attractive way to get attention, but with bling on its way out, you have to make your statement more demurely now. A museum watch piece like a Movado is always stylish. A single, elegantly placed diamond can spark a twinkle in her eye. Wearing a unique piece of art on your body may also attract hands for closer examination. But save your money. Don't buy new. Go to a pawn shop. There's no such thing as a "new" diamond. They're all recycled. A Movado at a pawn shop can also be 25% the cost of a new one, but there's with no discernible difference in quality. (NOTE: If you buy her jewelry, **don't** take her to the pawn shop.)

Cologne is okay if you have a signature scent, but mostly it just masks your body's natural pheromones, the chemicals that attract specific females to your body's chemistry. The products you use will have a scent, but other than that, go au naturel.

Do you have any idea how important dancing is? Some guys hate it even more than they hate watching me thrust into her, spank her buns to the beat, motorboat her décolletage, and dip her so I can kiss her stomach. So drink ten times more and practice at home in front of the mirror. Then take salsa or hip-hop lessons, and go to far-away bars where you can practice your moves in front of people you'll never see again. If your ego is too macho to boogie oogie oogie, then the boss (i.e., your penis) is going to have to schedule a meeting to discuss the communication breakdown at corporate (i.e., your brain).

If that all seems like a lot of work, then here's a man break for you: get some new porn. Don't watch it obsessively, especially if you have an addiction to it already. Instead, watch specific types that may aid your future efforts at threesoming. MMF, FFM, and FFF scenarios can be educational, not just prurient. Revel in the pleasure given. Observe almost clinically the moves the bi women make, and you'll become a better lover yourself when you trial-and-error all that you've learned.

While you're watching, ask yourself, *Can I do that move? Can I catch her rhythms like the lesbians just did in that scene?* You'd better have some tricks up your sleeve because when you have two naked chicks in front of you, you're going to have to do more than point at your erection like a caveman. If you're decent looking, caring, and rugged enough, some women are going to make you their sex toy when they tire of the vibrator, so make sure you have STD checkups every month if you rock, three times a year if you only rock a few weekends, and once every year if you're in a rocking chair. Because this is how women prepare for a ménage à trois: Step 1: Find a guy. Repeat. Quest over.

What skills do you have to offer in bed? Can you have multiples? Are you super long? Do you have a fast tongue? Maybe you have G-spot-shaped cock? Can you go all night without help from Viagra? There are books that will teach you sexual bravado. Masters and Johnson offer many guides, and so does Kinsey. There's so much to learn about the flow of semen, the role of the prostrate, tantric sex, penile exercises to increase rigidity and ejaculation strength, pros and cons of prescription meds, and even supplements to increase performance. The following is a simple, non-scientific methodology that will enable you to achieve one of the most sought-after skills in a man—the multiple "O."

Multiple orgasms aren't just for women anymore. Multiple means consecutively firing, not having numerous orgasms over the course of the night with breaks in between, although those are good for everyone too. And I'm not talking about sexing her for hours straight without losing rigidity. There are basic and advanced lessons you can learn for control. The sitcom way is to think about baseball players or grandmas or dead childhood pets. The modem way is, as it always was, through mind control. In case you forgot, your brain is still the organ in charge. You may have to do some re-training, but the women will appreciate your efforts. They always appreciate the effort. They reward the successes though.

During playtime with yourself, stroke it until the first ejaculation **but** don't release fully. Let the first two-thirds out leaving some "in the tube." Use the same muscles that you pump with to maintain the erection without additional stimulation. Hold that as long as you can using your fantasies, memories of ex-girlfriends, visual stimulation, and dreams of Scarlett Johansson's thunderous jugs quaking in your face. Can you hold it stiff enough to last through the next one? When you finally start losing the erection, manually stimulate yourself again back to rigidity, and repeat through the second ejaculation, again leaving remnants in the tube for the third ejaculation, and so on. You may reach seven orgasms or more in a day.

You can also train your dick to jump. The same muscles that push the semen from your testes into the shaft and then out the head are responsible for the jumping, which is actually pumping. Squeeze your butt cheeks together. Practice making it jump by flexing those muscles in your groin area. Imagine you're coming dry heaves. The harder and faster you can perform this, the more satisfying you will be on your second or third ejaculation, when it really matters in a threesome. The longer you can hold it in, the further it will fly (maximus velocitous), like shaking up a soda pop.

There are many resources on penis ENLARGEMENT. The internet *might* have a result or two, but I doubt it. I mean, who wants to enlarge their penis? Well, try anyway. Type into your search engine "penis enlargement." You're probably wasting your time though. It's just not in demand. I guess the world doesn't want any more big dicks in it.

2

WHAT: GETTING CHICKS = NUMBERS GAME. THREESOME = LOTTERY WIN!

IF YOU KNOW it's gonna happen for sure, then you don't know women. Women run sex. It's their cottage industry—recession-proof and drama filled. If you let them drive, they'll take you to the spot. If they leave you feeling like, *Wow, is this really going to happen?* then you're in the right place. Now would be a good time to shut up for the rest of the night.

So much of attraction is advertising and response. We men are visual. We're ocularly perceptive because traditional hunting involved identifying the prey before it identified you. Just like women today. We're attracted to their ponytail bopping around, big earrings, jiggling breasts, or the reflective shine from her pantyhose. In contrast, women are aurally perceptive because they bonded with each other and the children in the cave. There was no internet or Blackberry connection to find out where their men were with dinner. Just like men today. They subsist on compliments, communication, adoration, and sincerity—things expressed through words. Are you getting this, caveman? Advertising and response.

If not, then let's make it simple. The first part of this chapter includes things you should say. The second part of this chapter includes things you shouldn't say.

Guys always ask me why I'm so comfortable with women even though I'm not the model type. And how do I get all that "kablinky?" I tell them I used to do stand-up comedy and had to make connections with 300 people, so talking to only four or five women is easy. The point is, think big. You practice for threesomes all the time when you go out and talk to multiple prospects, but usually you only wind up sleeping with one. I want you to think four or five women, then settle for sleeping with two.

A great opener that doesn't rely on humor is the settling of a dispute (fabricated or not), a bet, or an argument that you just happen to need a stranger's opinion about. Lo and behold, there she is. I haven't met a woman yet who doesn't have an opinion about everything, so she'll be sure to share it with you. Watch her eyes as she interacts with you. If she's scanning, she's not that into you, so treat her like practice, then go. Don't take it personally. She might have a friend coming later who might be interested in you, unless you were a self-serving jerk earlier in the night and bitterly said after a rejection, "I'd take you home, but we already have enough pigs and cows on the farm."

Do give a nickname to the woman you've set your sights on. When she finishes a light-hearted story or does something embarrassing, work in an endearing moniker. It conveys your interest in a non-sexual way. Unless the nickname is sexual. Say something like, "Sure, sure, just ask *Rocket Fuel* here. She'll tell ya."

Here are some opening lines I've used consistently and with gratifying results:

1. "Hi, I'm (name). I do some publicity for the bar. Are you all having fun? ... Great, later we can all take a group picture. Maybe it'll make the (local) paper."
2. "What a fine-looking group of ladies. I've only seen more beautiful women in my own family's photos."
3. "Do you want to dance? I've been practicing my shimmying and jazz hands?"
4. "I like your _________." (something specific, and include a word about why it's unique on her.)
5. "Do yo man know you out looking this hot?"

Asking the right questions while flirting gives you insights into her mindset. Only ask one identifying question or it sounds interrogatory. The rest should loosen her up. Here are some questions I use:

1. "So, anyway, who do you do? I mean *what* do you do? *What. What.*"
2. "Why do you usually dump your boyfriends?"
3. "What's the worse date you've ever been on?"
4. "What would you do for a Klondike bar? Not that I have one."

(TIP: Whatever she doesn't like about her ex, you're Opposite-Man, superhero to the despondent bitches all over town. Bitches? Hey, you're a superhero ... you gotta have an attitude.)

When they ask you questions, most will be identifiers. The more identifiers they ask you, the more you're being weeded out. So get in the habit of driving the topic away from you and back to them or to the threesome. Use synonyms like "ménage," "tryst" and "chickee chickee wah wah." Then drop it like it's hot. Letting them bring it up indicates interest and, thus, qualifies them. If they don't, no chickee chickee. No wah wah.

Your answers to their questions about group sex should leave them feeling:

1. Curious
2. Embarrassed
3. Compelled
4. Disgusted
5. Empowered
6. Safe
7. Challenged
8. Horny
9. Wet

We can direct the responses to the questions creatively. They'll come randomly. Here are questions that correspond with the feelings above:

1. "Oh, you want to know how it started? It's a great story. Let me tell ya after I get a drink / go to the bathroom / make a phone call (or any other delay tactic)."
2. "No, they picked me, really. They were the ones totally in control. I was simply minding their own business, and they took me home. They made the moves. They got the multi-O's."
3. "One of them said that guys couldn't make her come. She told me what to do. I did it. She came. The end. Well, then she made me do it again four more times. The end."

4. "How can you say you're good in bed if you can only satisfy one at a time?"

5. "No I wasn't scared. They felt safe with me, and vice versa. We went to their apartment. They drove, and our friends all met each other. We just wanted to have some fun. I mean, I'd stalk them, but who has the time these days?"

6. "If you haven't done it yet, what are you waiting for? Why deny yourself the heady pleasure of having four hands exploring you or two tongues at once, finding all your secret places?"

7. "I'm one of those guys who can stay hard even after I bust one off and keep going all night, sometimes even after I bust the second one off."

8. "I wanted to do it before I was too old and nobody wants me anymore."

9. "The hottest thing is watching the straight woman go bi right in front of your eyes."

Now explain that it's your turn to ask the naughty, naughty questions. Here are some good places to start:

- In a 24-hour period, you can have ___ orgasms.
- The most public place you ever did it is __________.
- The most whore-ish thing you've ever done was __________.

- My secret sexual skill that nobody knows about is

  __________.
- If you're close to climax and he __________, you
  come right away.
- ___ percent of your sex life is one-night stands or
  flings.
- I am / am not wearing underwear right now.

If either one of the women brings up her children, say something like this:

- "No way you have kids. You look too young to even
  get pregnant."
- "All the other moms must hate how hot you are."
- "I'd love to meet your children someday."
  (TRANSLATION: Since I'll probably never see
  you again, I'd love to meet your whole damn family).

When is it okay to unload on a prospect? When she's any one
of the following, which are all really the same thing:

Mean Girl = Bully = Bitch

You should avoid her because it's impossible to beat her. The
most you can hope for is a superficial wound (for a superficial
woman). Try saying something like this:

- "Big butts are definitely in, honey. But not big thighs."
- "What university gave you that master's in bitchyness?"

You can't be friends with everybody. Most of 'em aren't worth your time. Personally, I love it when women weed themselves out for me. I used to get frustrated, but now I know that it's a blessing (albeit in disguise). Salad oil and vanilla ice cream don't mix well either, even if e-Harmony says vinegar ice cream is a match based on twenty-nine dimensions of personality blah blah blah. Congratulations. We're so happy for you. $59.99, please. (NOTE: It costs $720 minimum per year to use that dating site. That's before you even spend one dime on all your matches, women who can't get a date in the real world and don't know how to turn down a free meal.)

Here's how not to ruin a good thing:

- NEVER, NEVER, EVER go anywhere with strangers without telling a friend or taking a picture of them, their license plate, or their driver's license.
- Never acknowledge that it's going to happen until the decision has been made.
- Never say, "Let's have a threesome ... me and your two boobs."

- Never talk about your interests: sports, politics, news, religion, mom, or an ex.
- Never stare. Make a damn move or get out of the way so the other losers can.
- Never insult, ridicule, neglect, or intimidate the betas. They're your barometer.
- Never get caught in a lie. But you should definitely lie. Women want a man they can trust.
- Never tell her that she looks like someone else. Let her volunteer that info. Then follow up with some line like, "Scarlet Johansson, huh? I'm not seeing it. You're way hotter than that old cow."
- Never rely on your buddies to get you laid. They'd rather pirate your booty.

3

WHO: MY WIFE THINKS YOU'RE CUTE ... WHAT?!

THERE ARE many types of threesomes. Which one will happen on you?

- FFM – Two straight women and one guy (you get shared by two women; no bi action)
- FFM – One straight women, one bi woman, and one guy (you all get shared; includes bi action)
- FFM – One lesbian, one straight woman, and one guy (you and a lesbian share a straight woman)
- MMF – One straight woman and two guys (you and a guy share a straight woman)
- FFM – Two lesbians and one guy (maybe they'll let you watch?)

Each configuration has its own parameters, which you'll discover on your own ... hopefully. Certain facets of each can't be ignored. For example, are these people new acquaintances or old friends from college who all take ecstasy one night? Is this an established couple, like boyfriend / girlfriend? Is someone involved a married cheater? Each has varied requirements for fulfillment, expectation of outcomes, and differing solutions to the conflicts that arise, so be flexible. You know what I mean by that.

Husband & Wife (Swingers)

I introduced the couple with the pseudonyms "Manny" and "Laura" in the beginning. She's the reason you must charm every woman you meet and make her feel special. Eventually, married women cheat. Some just do it in front of their husbands.

"She's a real cutie you got there," you say to a woman holding an infant. When she thanks you, add, "No, I was talking to the baby."

When swingers invite you into their home, you must know that you're walking into history. These people have a past together. Tell her in a matter-of-fact tone what a lovely home she has, how stylish it is, how much you love the furniture, and, lastly, how much you want to stick your tongue all the way up her lady business.

The hubby will put up with you banging his horny wife but not with disrespecting her. So you should treat her like a million-dollar treasure. Service her when she throatily admits she likes to have her pussy eaten. Suck her hard nipples until she begs you to suck them more. Grab her hair, make a pony tail out of it, and drive her around the bed until you hear that familiar groan coming from her. Pretend you're a ravenous sex monkey who hasn't been fed in months. Pretend? Pretend nothing, monkey boy.

Let the husband do the honors of getting her started. He can slip her dress off. You might undo her garters. He can free her tits from her bra. You can suck one. From there, just do what you're told. She may want to have one of her fantasies fulfilled by two men. I'm talking, of course, about double penetration—one up front in her cunt and one en route, in her fruit chute (as explained to me by a porn star). (NOTE: **Never** come in a married woman. Even with a condom. Pull out!)

If you brush his hairy thigh during this exercise, don't freak out. You're not bisexual now. This sex is for her. It's hard to perform. Once she orgasms, you can concentrate on just satisfying her in turns. (NOTE: 90% of married men aren't gay. The other 10% aren't running around having threesomes that involve women anyway, so you're in the clear on the bi fears there, captain.)

Married swingers enjoy more discretion than couples that swing, so keep it quiet and she'll keep it poppin'. Chances are good that the wife will prefer familiarity over freshness, but don't let anyone fall in love. Then you'll have a love triangle, the lead indicator of a failing marriage. You're not there to bust up families … just her ass.

During my re-match with that couple, she started to catch feelings until I steered it back toward their intimacy. Sometimes you have to play marriage counselor. Like the first time we were together, I was being used as a conduit to spark a marriage that had gotten mundane. She confessed to me that she dresses all slutty because Manny likes it. She's okay with it, she guesses. The second time we all rendezvoused, Laura was pissed at Manny (infidelity?), so he brought me in to smooth things out. She was only giving me attention, alienating him, leaving him ashamed or neglected, so I had to intercede.

I gave her three O's (one all over my hand, one all over my face, and the last all over my cock), and she relaxed her attitude, so I convinced her to bring him back in because I'd be damned if this motherfucker is going to be a home-wrecker ("motherfucker" as used figuratively and literally in this illustration). That ploy worked well because he apparently learned his lesson. She became affectionate and enthusiastic for him again. When I snuck out the foyer soon after, they were still rocking in the bedroom.

Can you imagine if I'd hogged all the wifely poon to myself? It would have been like she was cheating on him right in front of his face. I wish I could say I acted as the glue that kept their marriage together, but they're divorced now. To be honest, it's healthier that way—from their perspective and mine. I've since seen the breathtaking Laura once since then, and she was in love with a new guy. I could see it in her eyes. I couldn't have been happier for her. And for the first time, she was dressed like a lady—a beautiful, distinguished lady.

Boyfriend & Girlfriend

In this scenario, eight out of ten times the girlfriend is the one (see POA) who invites an additional woman into her bedroom because three ain't a crowd. So here's my advice on this brand of threesome:

If the relationship is temporary – DO IT!
If the relationship is committed – DON'T DO IT!

Chances are good that you'll remember your first tryst much more often than Prudence Padooka, so be open-minded and ready. Later on, you can tell your friends, "She was the woman of my dreams ... but I have a lot of dreams, sometimes twice a night."

What about the times the boyfriend wants to invite an additional girl into the bedroom? Should he pick her? NO. NO. NO. NO. NO. NO. NO. NO! *She* definitely should. His best bet is to intimate that he doesn't even need it. He can plant the seeds in her mind like this: "I wouldn't want to bring another woman into our bedroom. It wouldn't be fair, and not for the reason you think. It wouldn't be fair to *her*. ... Me not being able to take my eyes off of you."

Always *make love* to your woman first. Then you can just *fuck* that other whore. The other whore will understand. Your girlfriend won't feel like a third wheel, and you might get to see some bachelor party action if you're lucky and your girlfriend is a freak like mine. You can initiate this at the strip club when you and your babe go out. See how far the stripper is allowed to go with your woman. If you catch her twisting on the dancer's fist, you might have a freak girlfriend. (TIP: Whether at the titty bar or in a threesome, don't ignore your woman. Otherwise this will be the last threesome you share, and there might not be any twosomes either, unless you count your two hands.)

Encourage your woman to experiment when it happens so you don't look too overeager in her eyes. You can say something like this:

- "Ooh, baby, you look so hot kissing her."
- "Let me rub your nipples while she's doing that."

Refrain, however, if the two ladies don't want to lez out. Let 'em work it out together.

To Bi, or Not Bi, That Is the Question (Their Giggles Are the Answer)

What about the two times out of ten when the girlfriend wants a second man instead of a woman? You have a few options in that circumstance:

1. It's been nice knowing you. Goodbye.
2. Okay. But I'm not getting involved.
3. Fine. But in return, I get __________.

Part of me would be concerned. Women's instincts center around nesting with one, strong provider. Someone who wants two or more men on top of her is missing something—passion, thrills, affection, love, adventure, or romance. There's a void that keeps getting refilled with the wrong, void-filling stuff. In other words, if there are intimacy or abandonment issues at play, beware. You should never take advantage of a woman.

I'll never forget my first threesome because one of the women had intimacy issues. My college sweetheart brought her girl-friend in to watch us have sex one summer day. I pounded her in a frenzy. She then offered me to her friend, who was reluctant to give it up because she was dating my roommate, who was an idiot. But she did regardless because I'd seen her nude in the shower accidentally a couple days earlier, so she figured well, the secrets are out ... and they were big secrets, if you know what I mean.

Her nervousness was obvious, and she had no orgasms (and I ate her religiously for twenty minutes before I slid it up her), so I remarked that she was sort of lousy in bed. The very next weekend, we left the university for her house, where they treated me to a sensational session of sexual bliss in the evening hours after many a drink. Without the worry of being caught by her man, she came through like a champ. The "lacking experience" strategy had worked.

The only problem was that I was falling for her and losing interest in my sweetheart. We all found ourselves at a party at my now-former girlfriend's house. Keep up. Like a jackass, I found myself in yet another threesome with her and my best friend in her bedroom! It gets worse. Just as my bud said to me, "Don't come inside her. I want to eat her out," in barged my ex-girlfriend with her new guy, screaming at all of us, "Get out! Now!" We did go ... eventually. But first we locked the door and finished. The joke was on my bud. I lied when I said I hadn't come inside her. Ha ha! (We're not friends anymore anyway.) The woman and I were establishing quite a pattern of debauched sex together, but she'd never do it alone with me. She also never talked to her best friend again.

It didn't end there. We threesomed again with another woman I'd been intimate with once but dumped because she had a list of things she wouldn't do. I thought they were pulling my leg or teasing me about doing it, but they showed up, shed their bras, peeled off their panties, and waited to see who I would fuck first. Like all encounters, everyone gets bug eyes watching the hot, hot action in person, especially if it's their first time seeing public sex.

So there you have it. The employment of multiple strategies (lacking experience, challenge opportunity, position of authority, and fear of something) enabled that daisy chain of free love during my sophomore year, which is also the year I learned that women like to have flings with nineteen-year-old boys. That was only a coincidence of sexual peaks, and we each probably thought the other was only good for sex. Looking back on it, my college sweetheart shouldn't have been showing my skills off to her friends. Women can't share.

Random Stranger Threesomes

This is the most common type of group sex. They occur everywhere—hotels, dormitories, frat houses, vacation getaways, or your rumpus room. Frequently, they involve two curious, experimental women who haven't gone bi ... yet. Sometimes a bisexual woman slips herself into the equation and makes things tricky. She could be using you as a catalyst to get a virgin, giving up her own ass to you for the opportunity. But when it comes to bisexuals:

> I don't trust 'em because they're having their cock and being eaten too.

The bi woman is aggressive, and in a ménage, there will probably be some girl-on-girl action first, so let them negotiate that. The straight woman wants dick for sure, but the bi woman might be indifferent. That indifference usually fades after two different people go down on her, then she might just have some of that dick after all, mister. If the straight woman refuses to experiment, let her know that it's okay just to watch or to come by herself. She doesn't have to do anything she doesn't want to.

With the straight women, it's quite straightforward. You womp them one at a time until they've had enough. They might kiss each other or jug-juggle each other's breasts, but don't expect too much more than that. Enjoy loving the ones you're with.

Orgies or Four-or-More-Somes

If you're not a rock star, a pro ball player, a pornographist, or Tom Sizemore, it's not easy to get invited to an organized orgy. Like most people who have participated in one have told me, they sort of just start on their own. But if you find your-self in one, use etiquette. Hooting and wooting is juvenile, so avoid that. Follow the group's lead, and don't push the envelope. As always, let the women determine when it's show-time. Let them move at their own pace, or you'll scare them off. If a woman says, "Hey *you*! Finger farm my asshole," you'd better get ready for a finger shower.

When it gets started full on, don't compromise the women. Move on when you're done, or stay 'til she says she's done. Wear condoms the entire time, even when you're cat-napping between loads. Be sexually polite. Ask her where it's okay to shoot it on her when it's time. (TIP: She has to keep looking good for the next few guys, so avoid her hair, eye makeup, lipstick, or pubic hair, if any. Aim for beige or pink.)

I cannot reiterate this enough: in any situation, group or duo, never ignore the betas. At the orgy, there might be a line to nail the hot chick, so warm up on the average women. They'll overcompensate for their smaller tits and bigger thighs by blowing the bejesus out of you. Use up your first milk bath on them because the second time you go, you can go for a while, which will impress the hot woman who has a smaller line around her now because all the selfish guys wanted to bust their first one on her hot alpha ass. Then maybe you come along and give it to her long enough that she can get off a gushy orgasm at the same time, and suddenly you're king.

4

WHERE: WHERE TO GO TO GET TO SECOND OR THIRD BASE IN PUBLIC? THE DANCE FLOOR

Women work out, buy trendy makeup, get liposuction, and alter their breast size because they're looking for someone to appreciate them in all the wrong places. Face it, you **don't** want to meet your soulmate while she's getting double penetrated by some bikers at a shroom fest. So how do you mine for qualified women? Where are they? We want a certain kind of woman, a threesome woman. Someone not typical. Someone with a colorful past. Someone who smiles at men a bit easier than the rest. Women without father figures. Hippy chicks, divorcees (but not widowers), single moms, middle children, bachelorettes, and the thirty to forty-five age demo— they all seem to be looking for more of a thrill than common women. Okay, widowers too. They could use some dick.

Real connections aren't always made in the dark, so go wherever women in your community go.

- NOT Curves women's only gyms
- NOT her gynecologist's office
- NOT the new lesbian support group.

What do you require from her? Beauty? Body? Behavior? Brains? Bucks? What combination of elements will satisfy your needs? Looks get the phone blowin' up, but brains keep it blowin' up. Then again, if she looks like microwaved ass left out in the sun too long ...

Beach. Boating. Bars. Concerts. Ball games. Soccer practice. Where are all the drunk women at? What's the difference (in odds) between a snooty martini bar and an urban country dive? None. There are tramp-ass sluts in both places. Each has its own culture, locals, attitudes, and value systems. And, of course, each one has a bleach-blonde bartender with a plunging neckline and tight black slacks that show off her sweet little ass.

All right, but what if none of this is well configured to your personality? What if you just want a threesome without *earning* it? You fantastic idiot of a man. Of course you can do that. We're men. We run this bitch.

Go directly to the source:

- Swingers clubs
- Nudist colonies
- Social events
- Personal ads
- Raves
- Las Vegas
- Escort services
- Women's prisons
- Women's colleges

Answer: Internet dating.

Question: How do women combine the two things they love most, shopping and dick?

Just as cosmetology is the new home ec, internet dating sites are the new personal ads. Women love the control, security, anonymity, and power they experience with this mating technique. I've personally tried a few services, and I've found that you can do better in close space than in cyber-space. Also, if you're a loser, you'll probably be an online loser, minus your money. But the thrill of the hunt is fun, and it's addictive to see who's matched to you or viewing one of your profiles.

So try your luck in person. On the weekends, try making real connections (not electronic ones) that are meaningful. Save the FarmersOnly.com losers for the throwaway weeknights.

Swingers Clubs

Swingers clubs offer more of a guarantee of group participatory sex. If you patronize events like "The Sex and So Much More Show" or "The Dirty Show" (as seen in metro Detroit), current information will be available. Any groups I disclose now could be raided by the time this book is published. There are actual vendors that will lead you into "the life" (that's what swingers call it) without going through some dirty bookstore or porn supply boutique.

Nudist Colonies

Nudist colonies tend to be a little more of a gamble. Nudism requires no clothing, a big plus for big people. The obese sweat in restrictive clothing and seek to free themselves of it at these locations. I'm not a chubby chaser, but if you are, this might be the way to go for you. That's about the only downside to colonies or resorts that are clothing optional. By their very design, they're amazing experiences for discovering your inhibitions related to your sexuality. The hairy muffs you see everywhere are the icing on the cake. So let them eat cake.

Social Events

LARGE-SCALE SOCIAL EVENTS like the Kentucky Derby, Ozzfest, or Puffy's party in the Hamptons (darling) are all excuses to party and hook up with a bunch of tipsy women. Wherever thousands of people gather to drink, you must be there to catch the little bonuses that elude us at smaller venues. The Burning Man festival is a drug-induced weekend in the desert that has tons of uninhibited women swinging their tatas proudly. Some even body-paint their breasts. Finger paint, anyone?

Then there's Mardi Gras. The Big Easy. The Mecca for the horn dog. The freest market of tits and ass in the United States. Everywhere you turn, tits, tits, and more tits. I like to flash my ass to bead throwers during the afternoon and collect premium beads to trade at night. Stuck-up women only flash for good beads. Fun ones do it for a ten-cent plastic piece of crap. Everyone does it because it's legal there. Just don't fight, piss in public, or pass out. Anything else is a blind pig, and the threesome juice flows freely. And cheaply.

Oh, did I forget to mention that you can take as many videos and pictures as you like (for private collections only) and that low-rider jeans and tops are dropping every second of the ten-day celebration? It's wonderfully weird when you see grandma and grandpa taking snapshots of whippersnappers and getting in on the fun themselves. If you can't have a threesome here, you can't have a threesome anywhere.

Vegas has the same vibe, except there are the zillions of cameras watching every breath you take. It's hard to strike out there, but if you do, remember that every day a million more girls turn eighteen. Look around you. Sex is everywhere in Las Vegas. It struts around the casino in thigh-high stockings and open-toed shoes. It litters the gutters with a million discarded porn flyers. It finds you when you win at the tables, and it bends over so far that you can see her belly ring down her blouse.

If worse comes to worst, you can hop on a party bus to visit the cathouses Nevada is famous for. Now is the time to bring up all your perverse idiosyncrasies. You wanna tickle a Jewish woman's nylon feet while a fat lady pops balloons with a cigar as another yells at you like your ex-wife in a pool of Jell-O pudding? This is your nirvana. Just expect to drop between $200 and $1,800 or more for the privilege. Also, hookers don't keep Snow White, Elvira, or Tinkerbell costumes on hand, so be courteous. Call ahead. (NOTE: You don't have to treat a whore like a queen in this instance. Just a whore.)

5

WHEN: WAKEY WAKEY BOOTY SHAKEY

MOST LOSERS HAVE the 300-date rule: if they can't sleep with her within 300 dates, maybe she's not worth it after all. The rest of us employ a three-date rule, which usually coincides with weekends. Friday night is statistically the best night for a threesome. The crucial hours are 10 pm to 1 am. But don't check the time while you're trying to land a threesome.

A typical woman with a shelf life won't waste time on nobodies, not when she wants to be married and happy like all her girlfriends (say they are). She has roughly eight hours per weekend to find Mr. Right in the booze-soaked cloud of men surrounding her.

Timing is more than that though. It's also about communication. We transmit billions of messages to each other, which divert us from our drive. Carrying the conversation is necessary while you're flirting, but you have to know how to listen. When my last girlfriend and I broke up, she said she needed closure. She meant of my mouth.

Despite her lies to the contrary, what she wants most of the time is your silence while you listen to her.

Timing is about knowing to hit the dance floor when you're asked or spontaneously meeting someone new. You don't have to dance all night, so have a good time while you're out there. Sense her closeness to you. Pay attention to what her eyes are doing, and give bad attention to any parts of her body requesting it. If she's rubbing all up on ya and gyrating that booty, she wants to feel your package. Spin her around, get behind her, and push it into her from the back while keeping the beat. We all tease one of my friends, Jerry, who seems to have multiple sets of hands that are always all over some woman's ass on the floor. Sometimes when he can't make it in person, he'll just send his hands along to grope all the ass being offered up.

If you worked it so you can sneak in a kiss on the floor, let her do the deep exploring. Keep it clean and sexy by keeping 80% of your tongue in your own mouth when French kissing. The tendency for men, who are often nervous, is to stomach pump her. Keep it short. There will be time for more off the dance floor. Hold the back of her neck as you kiss her, and make all the betas around the dance floor jealous when you wink at them watching you. You need the first kiss out of the way early. Ten million pounds of pressure usually accompany the first-date goodnight kiss, so bypass it quickly.

Your wingman's duties at 1:30 pm:

- Isolate the competition from you and the woman you've got your eye on
- Keep the betas drunk, diverted, and hooked up with others
- Provide the getaway car at the exit, ready to flee in case of last-minute competition
- Settle the tab, leave a tip, grab credit card and coats

After the sex, eventually all must leave to go home, sleep, and, more importantly, take a hot, soapy shower to put those strong odors down. Sometimes there's embarrassment, regret, or illness the day after, so don't be arrogant or a cad. And you can remind them how lucky you feel for experiencing that together, but ***never*** say thank you. You don't have to. They shouldn't either.

You may exchange numbers as a formality, but nothing usually comes of those contacts. Strangers sort of just go their own way. The likelihood of a re-match with the same partners is low (established couples are the exception). I usually say something like, "If y'all want, just booty call me. If not, that's all right too. But I'll never forget you two, especially tomorrow morning when I destroy my bedsheets thinking about it."

Most times, re-matches are just two one-night stands that happen to overlap (in more ways than one). While rare, a re-match can happen when one element in particular is present: ***trust***. I used an example of a re-union in the introduction to illustrate the sexual tension that trust was able to break. The anticipation was feverishly high as I wondered if they would offer a repeat performance. If that mix of lust and respect you brought to the last threesome was enough to earn you another golden invitation, then enjoy your encore.

If that sounds sappy, then you have to remember that it's their rules. Don't buy it? Go up to an associate at your company and ask him if you can bang his wife one night in his hot tub while the kids are away on a playdate.

Society—especially mothers—teaches women to let men approach them if they're interested. A woman who might let you spin her won't volunteer that or even make it easy for you unless and until she can get something from you. So what do you have to offer that's unique? They say women are the propagators of the species, but I challenge that notion. I say men are. Women just play defense. The sexes aren't better or worse than each other, just different.

The more time you take to understand and empathize with the other gender, the better off you'll be in a relationship, whether it's a threesome or a Mormon polygamist marriage (the ultimate orgy). Lust should never be underestimated.

Next week at the club, you'll hear the usual boasting, "I shot a forty-four at Braemar," or "I purchased an 85" UHD smart TV for the boat," or "My Testarossa just made *Car & Driver*." Poor you. Your only contribution is, "All I did was suck, fuck, and buck a couple of hot twenty-three-year-olds while their nail polish quivered off their toes. ... But TV sounds fun too."

6

WHY: THE WHYCOLOGY OF A THREESOME

WHY INDEED? Because two heads are better than one. Because four breasts are better than two. Because six holes are better than three. Or does the sway of the hypocritical, fundamentalist, religious extremists in our own country shame you into being a prude? I get it. You get it. Most people who can't have orgasms also can't get past their sexually repressed upbringings. As a result, they don't want anyone else having any fun either. You can see how little sense or credibility devout people have. When she's nude, she's beautiful, beautiful art. When it's another woman's naked body, it's filthy, filthy porn.

Why are women having more casual sex these days? There are many reasons for the higher incidence:

- *Sex and the City*
- Revenge
- Loneliness
- Children
- To be like men
- Empowerment
- Too busy for a relationship
- Escape
- Smart women making dumb choices (we'll explore that lie later)

You'd think that even for high-quality men, there is such a gender-wide rejection of men by women that they don't want "it." Blown off dates, fake cell numbers, shoot-downs, last-minute changes of heart—they're all really aimed at making sure she doesn't get the wrong "it." To get that tall, sexy, giant woman, you don't have to be:

A millionaire plastic surgeon to the stars, who models underwear on the side until his father, the king, dies and leaves him control of a small European country, where he has the largest recorded penis.

If you can merely discern what she needs and be her exclusive supplier of that need, she'll only have eyes for you. That's how you wind up with hotties and make everyone jealous.

Always be positive because your attitude is like sticky, connected taffy. It spirals positively or negatively, and once it gets going, it's hard to change the direction. Are you going to be this guy?:

"I've gotten hot women in the past, and I'll get another one. Maybe not this week, but soon."

Or this guy?:

"I had a hot woman, but now some other guy has her, and I have nothing."

7 Questions to Ask Yourself Before Your Ménage à Trois

1. What am I looking for? Lonely? Horny?Nympho?
2. What will I sacrifice doing this? Nothing?Respect? Reputation?
3. What do I want out of this? Orgasm? A story? Experience?
4. Am I taking advantage of someone, or is this mutual?
5. Is there protection?
6. Can they be trusted? Is this a setup of some kind?
7. Am I prepared to deal with contingencies if something goes awry?

If you don't have the answers to these question—and maybe some others—then now might not be the best time to engage in these behavioral dynamics. Conversely, if you're getting more putang than a teenage martyr in paradise, then maybe now isn't the time to psychoanalyze your issues.

Speaking of which, let's discuss this urban myth: ***smart women who make dumb choices***. Isn't that really just an enabling excuse made so women don't have to feel bad about themselves? Yes it is. Would those same women let us guys get away with excusing their behavior by saying that sometimes smart men make dumb choices? No they would not. They think we're all idiots. Just watch any product on TV advertised specifically to women. We're the idiots who have been running the world. So is this a hidden strategy?

Maybe. If you let her think she's making all the decisions, everyone's happy. Sound manipulative? If you said yes, you're getting closer to a threesome than you think.

Having a threesome isn't a dumb choice
unless you don't want it.

If you experience remorse, depression, shame, anger, or destructive thoughts, then you should avoid the patterns of behavior that lead to those feelings and seek counseling to sort through all those emotions.

I'm mainly talking to the women here but also to anyone who is sensitive. On the flip side, if you did nothing to contribute to its failure, don't blame yourself. There are a bunch of fucked up people out there. Some people think I'm one of them. Nah, they're just jealous. But sex changes everything. Just ask my maid.

If you're using women or men to ease your personal pain, then—on behalf of every person you use and leave a shell of their former self, making it that much harder for the rest of us —I propose that you go fuck yourself. That's pathetic. I'm talking to you gold-diggers, you snobby princesses, you phony rich chicks, you cocky frat guys, and, of course, your cheating ex.

Relationship vs. Threesome

Relationship

- You can establish yourself
- Love is possible
- You share each other's problems
- Satisfying but static
- It could last forever
- It could result in the blessing of kids

Threesome

- You establish a perception of yourself
- Love lands in her mouth and on her hair
- You share the whipped cream
- Rare but indescribably "undownlivable"
- So can you with a Viagra prescription
- Better not result in no blessing of no kid

A ménage à trois helps and hurts relationships. They're on a different level from just plain old infidelity. The roadblocks in a relationship are illuminated by feelings of neglect, jealousy, insecurity, etc., brought on by the outcome of the experience. Further, the closeness of the participants beforehand determines the long-term effects on them afterward. Strangers who play the game of tryster, on the other hand, often walk away satisfied, physically, morally, and emotionally, secure in the knowledge that no strings are attached.

A threesome is a mutually consensual, freely given exchange of lust. If you have to pay for it, it's not a threesome. It's prostitution, which is illegal in most states.

I'm not a doctor, but then I don't believe you need to be one to be an expert in relationships. My opinion should be part of a consortium of advice you consider as you make a plan that works for you. If you want to know how to have a good marriage, don't ask me. I'm single. I'm only an expert in the end of the old relationship and the beginning of a new one.

Disaster Scenarios (Avoidable and Fate-Driven)

Avoidable

- A better booty call comes up
- Somebody throws up / overdoses
- A fourth party barges in uninvited
- A parent or ex intervenes
- Someone passes out
- Not enough condoms or lube
- Somebody cries / freaks out

Fate

- A period suddenly starts
- A cell call from children / babysitter
- Someone dies / medical problem
- It starts a life-changing epiphany
- Jesus appears during your threesome

Pray he goes away. And keep me out of it. What threesome book? I didn't write no threesome book about extra marital affairs. Heh, heh. Nope that doesn't sound like me, Lord. Can I call you Lord? Great. (NOTE: If the deity makes his second coming in the middle of your first, please defer to the Christ figure or Buddha or whoever the real messiah is and allow him to have his way with your women first. It'll be the greatest sloppy seconds in the history of religion. Talk about holey.)

Too far? Too bad. Nobody's going to punish me for it because I don't believe in God, Jesus, unicorns, ghosts, or any other easy answers people cling to because they're scared of death. I believe in me. That power is mine inside, not at some extraneous structure I have to pay to enter. Prayer isn't magic. It's focused thinking. Grow up already. Really. Doesn't that make a lot more sense than excuses of faith? If you want to put your belief in something blindly, put it in the image in the mirror. Eating two women out in the same room at the same time doesn't make you godless. Posting someone else's picture as yours on Facebook makes you godless.

7

____

DURING: I DON'T EXPECT EVERY WOMAN TO SWALLOW ... JUST THE ONES WITH THROATS

THERE ARE a million ways to blow it and a few ways to get it right. Strip poker, truth or dare, spin the bottle, seven minutes in heaven, Twister—old school techniques to get women topless. Then came keys in a bowl. Now it's the internet.

Getting started can be nerve-wracking for beginners, which is why I recommend that you start kissing them both before you even leave for the love nest. You might be sweaty. You could have gas pressure building inside. You might get overzealous, or your timing could be off. Here's the solution to most of those problems: B-R-E-A-T-H-E. Breathe before your first big move when the bras simultaneously come off, when they both turn around for doggy style, when you're about to bust after ramming it home. Breathing does many things, including cooling your system down (so your endurance rises), focusing your mind (so you don't blow it), releasing toxins (from the chemical and hormonal responses in your body); steadying your blood pressure (so you don't die), and giving your lungs something to do (so they don't get bored).

Staying in the moment is important. You're all there. You all know what's going down. Now isn't the time to choke. Now isn't a good time to be pigging out in the kitchen or smoking pot, both of which could result in a pass-out situation.

Let the women giggle. They're nervous. They might spend some time in the bathroom preparing, so give 'em some time. If they're taking too long, you better go join the action, which might be starting without you. While that's happening, you might do some sit-ups, eat some dairy, take a vitamin E pill, breathe, take Viagra, and, ultimately, check you drawers. If they're not in display condition, toss 'em out her window and go commando. Marred underwear is one of the million ways to blow it.

Here are some ways to avoid distractions that kill the mood (be sure everything is prepared if it's your domain):

- Music on shuffle
- No TV
- Dim lights
- Candles
- Cell phones off

- Door triple locked
- Red light bulb
- Condoms

The tension before can best be described as "agonizingly sublime." The most common way to begin is by kissing each one and going from there. Some women are shy or inexperienced, and they take longer. Others go right for your cock. We call them single women, not freaks. I recommend that you let one of them pull out your schlong when they're ready for it. Women tell me they hate when a guy pulls it out and shoves it in their face. I guess that's why women wear so much makeup. Ya got shit flying at your face constantly.

Areas not to neglect on the female form: the nape of the neck between her ears and shoulders on the back of her neck. Small kisses along that strip will be greatly appreciated. When you move down to her chest, massage her chest properly. That's the area under her neck but above her boobs (they make a V). It's rarely done, but the muscles that hold those large tits up can be very neglected, then by the time you get to the nipples, all you have to do is blow on them once, and they should spring to attention. You told them you had skills, and now they want to see how skilled you are. Use all the erogenous zones. That's why there are so many.

Earlobes, the arch of the foot, the lower back. And, of course, what horny slut doesn't like having her toes sucked while she's being treated like a plastic love doll? Unless she hates her feet, then don't touch 'em.

If one woman is going to lick the other girl's truffala tree, great! If she's not, *nothing* you can say will make her ... unless it's about finding an 8 ball of coke. You're the guy. Of course you'd want to watch that, you perve. No, let them work out the squishy stuff. Chances are good it was already determined earlier that night. A threesome woman usually has some experience with both sexes, and she'll do all the leg work ... spreading them, that is.

I recall a woman in a hotel room once saying that she was going to close her eyes, and a tongue is a tongue. The bi woman looked at me for a millisecond before she dove into her pussy face first. The straight woman said she wasn't going to go down on the other woman, but she was wrong. After a blithering climax, she repaid the favor without any additional coercion from me. I had to push my eyes back into their sockets after watching that and roll my tongue back up and push it into my mouth. The thrill is watching the straight woman go bi right before your eyes.

The laws of chemistry cannot be denied. They cause you to favor one woman over the other, maybe because she has great big tits and you love tits and the other is as flat as a board. As long as the beta feels appreciated, that's all you can do. Try saying, "First you, then you, then you again, then you two without me, then all of us, and, finally, if there's time, none of us."

Using the line "then you again" implies repetition and quality on her part, leaving her feeling integral to the experience and not feeling like an ugly third wheel. You still have two women to satisfy, ugly or not. Two times the women = two times the pussy to eat. If you don't like oral sex, this is going to be one short, disappointing threesome.

If one of them is about to come, encourage it with nasty, dirty talk or by caressing and stimulating her tits. Whatever is inside of her making her orgasm at the time, tell her to come all over it. When you're about to come, you can put it two ways: I'm gonna or where should I? Pick one, depending on your style. Unless they're kinky hooker burgers, most of the time you'll explode into a rubber inside one of them. But if you get the opportunity to shoot a load for showmanship, make it the first and most impressive one. But check yourself. If you come all over her mouth, she might want to kiss you later. If it's on her tits, that gets sticky later on. If it's on her feet, you're one sick bastard, but I applaud your creativity. (TIP: A vibrating, battery-operated toothbrush makes for a nice substitute dildo.)

If they suggest costumes or lingerie, remember that pantyhose aren't intended for sexual misuse, but ... oh oh oh oh oh. Outfits and toys. That's what married women say keeps the sexual chemistry going. I don't often buy lingerie for my girl-friends when we're dating because should we break up, I don't want her wearing it for some other guy. But if I do, I sew in "PROPERTY OF MIKE GRANT" right across the cups.

Take that, jerk.

Fade out

APPENDIX
DETAILS: A THREESOME IS A GIFT, NOT AN UPGRADE

Things That Are Appropriate to Say

- "I'm the luckiest guy in the world, the state ... okay, the room.
- "I promised you ladies all twelve inches ... but you can only have three inches ... twice ... each."
- "This is even better than my last threesome ... I got **snuffed**."
- "Oh my (insert deity: God, Vishnu, Buddha, Alec Baldwin, whoever)."

Things That Are Not Appropriate to Say

- "Do you have any sisters who might want to join us?"
- "Your thighs look a lot bigger without those jeans on."
- "What's that growing on your _________?"
- "Can this count toward my community service?"

CONGRATULATIONS. At the conclusion of your first three-some, you will have attained one of the Top 10 most common male fantasies of all time. Look for further editions to aid you in these exploits. Now that you're hooked, I'm gonna really screw you on the price of the next book.

Rankings

10 – Two women at once

9 – Three women at once

8 – Two lipstick lesbians converted

7 – Two sisters

6 – Mother *and* daughter at once

5 – Old high school crush

4 – Trailer full of porn stars

3 – Teacher (middle school)

2 – Twins

1 – Scarlett Johansson

List For Emergency Preparedness

- Candles
- Wipes
- Lube
- Towels
- Antacid
- Cash
- MP3 player
- Aspirin
- Lighter
- Liquor
- Ice
- Mixers
- Red light bulb
- Hand sanitizer
- Decent conditioner
- Cold beer
- Toilet paper
- Dozen condoms
- Cigarettes
- Visine
- Fireplace logs
- Whipped cream
- Clean sheets
- Contact lens solution
- Vitamin E

- Drug dealer's phone #
- Häagen-Dazs (strawberry)
- Chaser supplement
- Flavored body lotion
- Any uniform
- Viagra, Cialis, Levitra
- Dimmable lights / lamp
- Porn DVDs
- Water bottles
- Large fruit / vegetables
- MAC facial cleanser

And, of course, don't forget the ***free movie passes*** ... for your roommate, so he can get the fuck out.

Things You Won't Be Needing

- Inflatable plastic love doll (Hey, let's make it a foursome)
- A gun (they're already here, man)
- Credit card
- Your buddies
- *Star Wars* figurines or anything that interests *you*
- Sex toys that wouldn't fit into an elephant
- Shrine to your ex-fiancé (temporarily remove that. You can always put it back up when you slip completely back into dementia.)

One last contingency to plan for is the abrupt exit strategy. For example, if something in her panties smells like a dying skunk fucking another deader skunk, haul balls!

Case Study: Swingers

"Whatcha doin', man? You still at that bar? Come on over. We're partyin' over here. My wife thinks you're cute."

I was there in 4.3 minutes, or 4.20 to be stone sure. Two other attractive women were chatting with his wife, Laura, a brunette, blue-eyed knockout. I couldn't get anywhere with either of them, but not for lack of charisma and charm.

Cut to the master bedroom. She was falling out of her flimsy white dress, and Manny pulled her tits out and asked me what I thought about them. "Not bad for a chick with three kids, huh?" She protested, and I thought it was going to end there.

"Damn, girl. You've got beautiful breasts," I blurted.

She shyly tried to cover one up, but her big pink nipple saw me. It was too late to pretend we were strangers. I dropped in front of her and nursed that soft flesh while she and her man made out. While I squeezed and shook her boob, she cooed and spread her legs open for me.

"She likes it when you eat her pussy," he said to me.

I immediately began fingering her under her little skirt. Then I went in face-first. I looked up, and she was giving him a hummer. He looked down at me and nodded. Unbeknownst to us, at that moment their last guest left, a door slamming shut after them. They likely saw us all fucking the hostess.

Oblivious to their drama, I threw her on her back and made her suck my big cock while I rubbed her pussy and her clit, finding her rhythm. She started heaving, then she held her breath and exhaled as she came all over my hand. I watched as he screwed her. He watched as I screwed her. I complied with all of her instructions. Hey, I'm a guest in their home.

She asked me to DP her with Manny. I was like, *Ummm*. But then she sweetened the offer.

"You can fuck me in my ass. I never let him do that to me," she said as she wiped my sperm droplets off her eyelashes and her cheeks. She licked her French manicured fingernails clean of my juice. I was instantly hard again. I'd left some in the tube, and I was up again, ready to sodomize the shit out of her ... or into her. I'm not sure how that goes.

It didn't work out well. It was my first DP, and the positions seemed hard to perform. It was fun, but not porn-movie fun. Not that I'm complaining.

I got to do her three more times over the next six hours, 'til morning, even after he passed out. She did some depraved things to me, and that's how I knew she was married.

When they walked me out into the bright morning sunshine at 6:00 am, the sun didn't blind me, as it usually does. It was freezing cold, but I didn't mind the chill, and I kept my jacket off. He asked me how I was doing. She smiled at me in her see-through negligee, her nips poking through the material. That lace didn't have a chance.

I was euphoric. She was a stunning 10+ with a 10+ body. It was literally like having sex with an angel. Dirty, humiliating, forbidden sex ... with a sweet angel ... who slutted her way into heaven because she was that good a slut. I wanted more. I wanted them to break up so I could have her to myself and live happily ever after. I was falling for a mom. So I never called them or went back to the same martini bar.

Until about three months later.

Case Study #2: Random Strangers

"You're funny," she said.

I pulled her closer and held her petite frame in my arms so I could whisper in her ear, "You're gorgeous, and you have an ass I could juggle. Now feel mine. I've been rollerblading."

She smacked it so hard. The whole bar turned to see if someone got shot or something. I mean, she cracked it so loudly that Helen Keller was like, "What the fuck was that?" And she's deaf and blind ... and **_dead_**!

I swiveled over to her girlfriend and said, "You can feel it too. But feel the right side, she shattered the left cheek."

She felt it more gently, prolonging it by continuing to rub my ass. I grabbed her and started making out a little. Her buns were so soft, a cross between a Jell-O mold and a loaf of white bread. The first one drunkenly, sloppily kissed both of us, forcing the triple kiss. By that point, people around us were taking notice.

"I thought you were going for that hockey player guy over there. And you were hot for that little freaky goth girl," I teased them. But I knew the faux set-up had borne it's rotten fruit, and I was about to make a fruit salad. "Do you really want to do it? I bet one of you will change your mind at the last minute."

"Not me," they said in unison. They both had that familiar devilish look in their eyes.

Cut to the apartment of one of the women. The obviously bisexual woman and I were working out the details in the kitchen, unaware that the other woman had stripped completely naked and was lying in the bedroom, her knees up, her legs spread. Entering the bedroom, we were both pleasantly surprised by the sight. We had expected her to be a little more work, being an alpha and all.

Her breasts were weird-looking B cups, but I told her how big they felt and how just looking at them got me all hard.

"Let's see," she said.

I slid my pants down, and my cock was standing up in my underwear, stretching it out like a circus tent.

"Ooh, he's got a big one. I wanna suck it," one of them said. (I'll let you guess which one.)

I pulled my mushroom head out of the top of the waistband and told her to kiss it if she wanted it to come all the way out. She licked and nibbled the tip, so I fed the whole thing to her while the bi woman was already mining for lesbians down in her crotch. Then I went down on her. To my surprise, the bi woman started deep-throating me. The straight woman bucked her hips into my face as she came all over the place.

The bi woman went back down on her after I did, and she made slurping noises as she drank the sticky juices. The straight woman started bucking again, and she had her first girl-girl orgasm. She wet the bed a second time.

"Eat my pussy, Mike," the bi woman said to me. "You won't make me come, but I still wanna see *your* skills."

I gave it my best effort, but she didn't have one ... yet. I could feel the straight woman putting a rubber on my very hard dick.

"Oh oh oh, no. I'm not fucking anyone until you eat her pussy." I was just kidding, but she pushed the bi woman down and began tepidly running her tongue over the unfolding folds. Occasionally she dabbed her clit. She was very stiff and had no confidence in what she was doing, but she tried. I knew the bi woman would come because she had a virgin under her, so I started twisting and sucking on her little tits. She loved it. Little tits are usually *very* sensitive.

"I can't believe you're still hard." She gasped as she slid into an orgasm.

"God, look what I'm looking at. I'm the luckiest guy in the ... room."

She didn't hear me. Her eyes were rolling around in their sockets as she shuddered one off. It was completely different from the first woman's O. The straight woman looked up at me with cunt juice all over her mouth, and I made out with her while she pulled my cock into her. I didn't do a thing as she wiggled and thrust all over it until she had another incredibly wet orgasm, which the bi woman was licking off my balls from behind me! That was it. I shot my second bucket of baby batter right up her.

Now here's the amazing part (as if it's not all amazing). I swapped for a fresh condom and started doing the bi woman before she could get dressed and leave, having got what she came for. She enjoyed it, but surely not as much as I did.

"It's okay, baby," she said. "It feels good, but guys just don't make me come. They can't hold it hard enough and long enough for me to work it."

I was like, "I see why. You have such a super tight pussy."

I stopped thrusting and froze in position. She bent over in front of me and started bashing her vag against my cock, which had not gotten soft over the last two hours. She was so violent and rigorous that I couldn't believe my ears when she let out a throaty "UUMMGGH!" Then she began shuddering, shaking, convulsing, and hyperventilating.

The other woman was half laughing, half worrying. I pulled out and stuck it in the straight woman again, who wanted to have another one "her way." She sat on me reverse cowgirl style, and I came insider her again before she could loosen one off. Now I needed a break.

The bi woman finally came out of her world and—shockingly—snuggled up to me on the bed. After peeing, the other woman joined us in our sweaty, musky little heap. We laughed and talked about it. They started playing with each other's tits, and I got excited again. The bi woman kept telling us that we'd just witnessed her most intense orgasm of her life. And it was from a dude of all people! The straight woman started stroking me, and then she popped me into her mouth. I rubbed her butthole, and she moaned, "No, no," so I squeezed her fine ass and fast fingered her. The bi woman rubbed herself as she watched us. This time she strung a condom on me and guided me into the straight woman while sucking her ample boobs and biting her nipples.

I wanted the bi woman's tight pussy milking my fast load, so I switched up and started hammering her until I couldn't take its vise grip on my dick anymore. My dick surrendered, fired its final shot, and deflated like Pauly Shore's comic theory.

"Okay, I gotta go to my boyfriend's, so everybody out," said the bi woman.

I didn't know which part of her statement was more upsetting: the fact that we were getting the after-sex boot or that she had a *boyfriend.*

The straight woman took me to her apartment, where we fell asleep together. She was the alpha. Let the beta go do her beta things.

The next morning, I woke up and slammed her into a dizzying oblivion one more time. That was my last condom left from a six pack. Umm.